CLARITY IS POWER

Q & A

"Clarity is Power" book series, is a collection of wisdom from thought-provoking Q and A with renowned Mahatria. His unique gift of answering questions spontaneously is captured in this book, offering life-changing insights.

The "Clarity is Power" series comprises 11 illuminating volumes, each addressing essential aspects of life:

1. Attitudes
2. Self-Discipline
3. Emotional Development
4. Relationships
5. Marriage
6. Parenting
7. Student Life
8. Career Growth
9. Leadership and Entrepreneurship
10. Spirituality
11. Faith

Mahatria Spiritualist | Thought leader | Diviner of infinitheism

For nearly three decades, Mahatria has empowered millions worldwide to achieve holistic abundance. His profound wisdom uplifts people in health, wealth, love, bliss, and spirituality.

infinitheism, the path divined by Mahatria, inspires breakthroughs for anyone who ardently desires abundance by transforming the human spirit to have faith in its infinite potential.

First published in India

MANJUL

Manjul Publishing House

• 2nd Floor, Usha Preet Complex,
42 Malviya Nagar, Bhopal 462 003 - India
• C-16, Sector 3, Noida, Uttar Pradesh 201301 – India
Website: www.manjulindia.com

Distribution Centres:
Ahmedabad, Bengaluru, Bhopal, Kolkata, Chennai,
Hyderabad, Mumbai, New Delhi, Pune

In association with:

infinitheism

3, 3rd Cross Road, R A Puram,
Chennai, Tamil Nadu, India
www.infinitheism.com

SPIRITUALITY (CLARITY IS POWER)

by

mahātria Rā

This edition first published in 2016
Third impression 2024

ISBN 978-93-5543-430-2

Printed and bound in India by Thomson Press (India) Ltd.

CLARITY IS POWER

Q & A

SPIRITUALITY

mahātria

CONTENTS

CONTENTS

1

Some say we are going to enter a spiritual era, and everything will change. Looking at the way the world is, will it happen? Such paradigm shifts on Earth, do they happen?

After three centuries of foreign rule, in a matter of decades, everything changed through one Mahatma Gandhi. For centuries they were enslaved, and in a matter of decades, everything changed through one Nelson Mandela.

The very fact that more people from Generation Y are taking up Yoga, Meditation and God than Generation X, is evidence that the trend is in that direction.

When a certain critical number achieves certain awareness, this new awareness gets communicated from mind to mind. A thought-level entrainment happens.

When only a limited number of people know of a new way, it may remain the conscious property of these people. But there is a point at which if even one more person tunes into this new awareness, a cosmic field is strengthened, so that this awareness is picked up by almost everyone!

Humanity at that point will go through a dramatic and collective shift in consciousness. It will happen when a shift is reached in the critical mass, when a certain number of spiritually awakened individuals happen.

Quantitative change brings about a qualitative transformation. Whether it is ideas or products or messages or behaviour... at the point of critical mass, it just spreads like a virus... as if a spiritual epidemic has happened.

The point of critical mass is that magic moment when it all begins to spread like wildfire... everything changes all at once.

When a certain critical number achieves certain awareness, this new awareness gets communicated from mind to mind. A thought-level entrainment happens.

mahātria

2

If He really loves us, then why such cruel times exist in our life ?

Didn't the earthquake in some part of the world result in the grave tsunami in so many other parts of the world? More people died elsewhere than where the source of destruction happened.

Having shrunk the world into an economic global village, though the epicentre of this economic-quake is in that 'land of opportunities', the rest of the world was feeling the tremors of the failures of their economic systems.

A human being's only fall back, God, is not without a cruel sense of humour. His *leela* doesn't necessarily make a human being laugh. Sometimes, His *leela* does make them cry. But then, there is no point in asking, why the scores in tennis are 15, 30 and then 40? Absolutely no point in asking, for that's how the rules are and that's how tennis is played. What's the rationale behind 'Love all'? Why 'Love - 40'? No point in asking - that's how the rules are and that's how the game is played. The passionate game-lovers don't think the rules are foolish, but will call you a fool for questioning them.

If this is with man-made games, what's there to speak about His-games? He has this cruel sense of humour in playing His *leela* in ways that a person is tested and challenged, time and again, and again. It is futile to question the game. Instead, learn the rules, master the game, play it well, and win the game.

There is one rule in His game that comes to our rescue - the end is always beautiful and it is in our favour. Know from the beginning that the end is always beautiful. No parent will ever give the child a story to read, which doesn't have a happy ending. Derive strength from knowing this and play the game courageously. Play it with strength. ●

It is futile
to question the game.
Instead, learn the rules,
master the game,
play it well,
and win the game.

mahātria

similar events; it becomes so evident that life is struggling to teach a below average student who is refusing to learn anything from the procession of events he has been bumping into. Hey, growth is caught, not taught. The school of life uses experiences as its teacher to help us mature but if we refuse to catch growth, we then put even life into a helpless situation.

A man met God and asked "What does it mean to be born?" and God replied "Experience it and you will know." He further asked, "What does it mean to grow as a child?" and God replied "Experience it and you will know." He further asked, "What does it mean to be an adolescent?" and God replied "Experience it and you will know." He further asked, "What does it mean to work and be rich?" and God replied "Experience it and you will know." He further asked, "What does it mean to get married and have children?" and God replied "Experience it and you will know." He further asked, "What does it mean to age and die?" and God replied "Experience it and you will know."

A little annoyed, the man asked, "If I have to experience everything for me to know what it means, then God, why are you there?"

God compassionately replied, "My son! Experience is my other name."

*Life is something of
what happens to you
and everything else of
how you respond to it.*

mahātria

4

I pray to my lord
every morning.
That is 'Prayer in life'.
I hear you say
'Life is a prayer'.
How do I grow from
'Prayer in life' to
'Life is a prayer'?

Coordinating the resources in a certain order to serve a specific function is called work. Bringing the fingers together in a certain order to hold a pen and then moving the hand in a certain order is writing. Directing the mind in a certain order is thinking. Mobilising the tongue in a certain order is speech. Coordinating the body, mind and emotions in a certain order is action. Coordinating action to serve a defined objective is work.

So, work is effective management of resources in a certain order to achieve a specific, functional objective.

While all the resources of our life are God's gift unto us, the work we create out of all these resources is actually our creation. True, the flowers, the fruits and the air we have to articulate to pray in words are all His. Even this very me/us is only His. But the work we create out of all these resources, including us, is our creation.

Let our prayer be, "Oh Lord, all the work I do is my creation, of course out of your resources... but it is my creation. From now on, I shall no more pray to you in words, nor perform any rituals. I will not offer you flowers or fruits. However, all the work I do from now on will be my offering unto you. Lord, because I offer you nothing but the best, all the work I do from now on will be nothing but the best. They say, everything that we have in life is your gift unto us. True, my Lord, but I also say unto you - everything I do in life will be my gift, my offering, my expression of gratitude unto you."

The disciple asked the Master, "Now that you are enlightened, what do you do in life?" The Master replied, "I draw water from the well and chop wood." The disciple again asked, "Before you got enlightened, what have you been doing?" The Master again replied, "I used to draw water from the well and chop wood." Puzzled, the disciple commented, "There seems to be no difference in your life, before and after enlightenment." The Master smiled and added, "There is no change in my actions, but the quality with which I perform my actions has completely changed."

Some people meditate in life. For some, life itself is meditation. Some people pray in life. Let the very life we live become our prayer unto Him. ●

❝

All the work I do
from now on will be
my offering unto You.

mahātria

How does it feel to be
deeply connected to God?
What happens to our life?
What happens to us?

A group of politicians and their followers had barged into my office one day. They wanted funds for elections. I politely explained to them that we do a lot of good to the world directly, and we wish to use our funds for such purposes and not for any political reasons. Some of the followers reacted in extremely disrespectful tones.

I looked straight in the eye of the political leader, who had led the crowd into my office, and asked him, "If I tell you, I personally know the Chief Minister of the state, will you still behave the same way?"

A little startled and with a quiver in the voice, he asked in return, "Do you know the Chief Minister?" I replied, "If knowing the Chief Minister of the state makes one so powerful, how powerful must I feel, for I know God personally?"

You cannot control a man who knows no fear. They saw fearlessness in my eyes and quietly left. That's how you feel when you are deeply connected to God. You feel when God can be with us, who can be against us. You feel God is your shield.

My mother had suffered cerebral haemorrhage, which triggered a heart attack. At the age of 69, after undergoing a massive surgery and then three weeks in CCU and ICU, she was critical. Around the same time, I had my spiritual retreats and over a hundred people had converged from all over the world for the retreat.

During the retreat, everyone is cut off from the world outside, and no form of communication is allowed with the world or from the world under any circumstances.

Krishna tells Arjuna, "Do not bring in your personal emotions on the way of executing your duties and responsibilities."

My predicament was the same. Either stay back as the son of my mother or go to the retreat as the teacher of hundreds. For me, both were my personal emotions and both were my duties.

If out there I take people closer to God through various spiritual practices, I had this unquestioned faith in the heart of my hearts, that God will represent me out here and take care of my mother. I went ahead with the retreat.

Faith always unfolds miracles. On the same day I returned from the retreat, my mother got discharged and she returned home. The more and more I do God's work,

I have personally seen, the more and more God does my work. That's how you feel when you are deeply connected to God. You feel God is in your team.

Staying close to fire keeps you warm. Walking through fresh breeze, you feel refreshed. Being in running water you feel clean. Stay long enough in a rose garden and you start smelling like a rose. You inherit the traits of what you are connected to.

Similarly, when you are deeply connected to God, you feel purified. In your thoughts, in your feelings and in your consciousness, you feel so pure. The drop of water falls into the ocean and becomes the ocean. You dissolve and you evolve. You disappear and God appears.

In all, by being deeply connected to God, experience after experience, you experience the deeper, higher and the beyond dimensions of life. ●

6

When does the life of a human being become complete?

As much as communication with the world outside, the quality of communication with your own self is equally important. It is by the quality of communication we have with our own self, our conscious mind trains our subconscious mind to believe in something. Prayer, in fact, is as much a communication from your conscious mind to your subconscious mind, as much as it is between you and your God. You derive maximum benefit from this system of self-communication, also called autosuggestion, by holding a given thought in your mental focus and by excluding all other thoughts, by repeating it in a relaxed state, constructing it with positive assertions, visualising it happening in your life as you verbalise, making it progressive, adding emotional content, and communicating in the present tense.

One such self-communication that can have a holistic impact on your life is, "Day by day, in every way, I am becoming, Most and more, healthy, wealthy, loving, blissful and spiritual."

Day by day: Growth is an everyday affair and not a 'once in a way' affair. Every today has to be better than yesterday and every tomorrow should be improved upon today.

In every way: Growth has to be multi-dimensional. Success in one role is no compensation to being a failure in another role. It is not enough being a one-role wonder. The focus is on being a holistic wonder.

I am becoming: Live with verbs and not nouns. Instead of I love you - I am loving you, instead of I like growth - I am growing, instead of I have learnt - I am always learning, and instead of I have arrived - I keep arriving... life is flowing and so shall we. Living has to be in present continuous... So, I am becoming...

Most and more: Contentment doesn't mean I settle for less. Contentment only means I will enjoy what I have, with no regrets or complaints. Existence is designed for abundance and not scarcity. You draw abundance in all forms by being abundant-conscious. Spell life as M.O.R.E. You deserve Most and more.

Healthy, Wealthy, Loving, Blissful, Spiritual: All that we need to achieve can only be achieved through this vehicle called body - so healthy; financial abundance in the hands of a good human being will build a better world - so wealthy; the emotional need is to love and to be loved - so loving; divinity waits at the door of a happy soul, and what's not happiness cannot be God - so blissful; and a human being alone can self-realise the divinity within - so spiritual. Only in fulfilling all these five needs the life of a human being is complete.

“

Contentment doesn't mean I settle for less.

Contentment only means I will enjoy what I have, with no regrets or complaints.

mahātria

7

> *Spirituality and spiritual masters world over, advocate contentment. You always speak about abundance, Most and more..., and wealth creation. What sort of spirituality is this?*

First and foremost of all, do not expect conformance from me. George Bernand Shaw said, "The reasonable man adapts himself to the world; the unreasonable one persists in trying to adapt the world to himself. Therefore, all progress depends on the unreasonable man." He also said, "You see things and you say 'Why?' But I dream things that never were and I say 'Why not?'" I am unreasonable, and I always ask, "Why not?" So, don't except conformance from me. Revolutions don't happen by endorsing what already is. Revolutions happen when things that never were begin to happen. And, we are here to cause a revolution.

Secondly, to treat spirituality and materialism as two opposites is utter ignorance. In fact, every spiritually aligned place, spiritually aligned institution, and spiritually aligned individual has magnetised abundance. They may not have used that wealth for themselves; they may have used it for the larger good; but the truth is, spiritual rootedness does magnetise abundance.

Thirdly, no religion advocated paucity. Unfortunately, religion is always used as a context to advocate scarcity. The son of a king should not be a beggar. As children of that Omnipresence that represents abundance, we should not be living within meagre means. Contentment doesn't mean you shouldn't be ambitious. Because like begets like, it is necessary to be abundant-minded to draw abundance. Scarcity-minded people are always aware of what they lack. So they draw more scarcity into their life. We can be abundant-minded by being grateful for what we have. No matter how little we have, we are rich, if we are grateful. No matter how much we have, we are poor, if we are ungrateful.

A heart laden with gratitude need not go in search of abundance. Instead, abundance will flow into our life. So, contentment only means, "I will gratefully cherish what I have without any regrets." As long as I cherish what I have with no regrets and continue to strive for more, I can be ambitiously contented.

Our thoughts create our reality. We get what we focus upon. In any situation, we see what we expect to see. Nothing will be ours unless we are convinced that it belongs to us. We deserve abundance. There is always a war between the contentment of 'From where to where?' and the ambition of 'From here, where?' While contentment does not challenge your potential, ambitions do. So, let your ambitions win over your contentment. Make your potential count.

Seek Most and more from life. Seek abundance. You deserve abundance.

Finally, to your question, "What sort of spirituality is this?" Every spiritual revolution is nothing more than timeless wisdom repackaged in contemporary language to enable the humanity of that time to adapt to it. Then, infinitheism is contemporary spirituality that's born to enable this generation to adapt to the timeless wisdom, which truly borders on abundance and not scarcity. My friend, 'This' and 'That' is possible... Come with me...

I think I have a spiritual streak in me. I want to live as a renunciate, but I am equally scared, what will I do with my life after giving up everything else?

First, give up this thought that you can embrace renunciation by decision. Renunciation isn't a decision. In fact, renunciation cannot be a decision. You actually grow into it. The egg does not decide to become a chicken… it grows into a chicken. We see the shell falling apart and the chicken emerging. We see only one moment, but the defining moment is the culmination of a series of momentary growths. So is renunciation. Renunciation is not what you think, for that matter not what most of the world thinks, a give up. You give up nothing. It is the immature mind that says, 'He renounced his sleep to embrace exercise'.

In reality, when someone's attachment for health becomes greater than their attachment for sleep, they give up a lower attachment in order to embrace a higher attachment. Renunciation is not a give up… it is a go up. Renunciation is metaphorically similar to a person climbing a ladder. They step off the lower rungs of the ladder because of their inclination to step into the higher rungs. They are not giving up the lower rungs. They are, as a matter of fact, going up the higher rung.

Simply put, at every given instant, life offers you the choice between the lower and the higher in every aspect of life. Use your intelligence to discriminate the lower from the higher and now wholeheartedly desire the higher. Like the child who automatically outgrows its attachment for the existing toy to a more exciting, new toy, your inner being will evolve to renounce the lower and embrace the higher. Then, life will never be a give up for you but a never-ending sequence of go ups.

Start from where you can start. Desire health... desire self-mastery... desire willpower... desire progressive attitude... desire them all so much so that you outgrow all the self-created hurdles that are preventing you from achieving what you want. Even this is renunciation. The more and more you discriminate between the lower and the higher, and embrace the higher... your life will graduate into a state of selflessness. You will begin to think beyond yourself. It is not that you won't have goals any more, but your goals will be more in the larger interest rather than being merely self-centred. This very progression is spiritual evolution... the spiritual realm is not at the other end of the materialistic realm... the egg and chicken are not at opposite ends but are a natural progression. So renunciation isn't a destination, but a path to the higher... ●

"

Renunciation is not a give up...
it is a go up.
Renunciation is metaphorically
similar to a person climbing a ladder.

mahātria

9

Do 'I lead my life'
or
is my life 'being led'?

Life is like a game of chess. You play this game with a partner called God (Existence). One way of looking at the game is that after every move of yours, God makes a countermove. But, you can see it in another way too. After every move of God, you can make the countermove. God's move was that Milton became blind; but Milton's countermove was to write one of the greatest expositions on nature - Paradise Lost. God's move was that Beethoven became deaf; but Beethoven's countermove was creating some of the world's greatest symphonies.

Legends like Helen Keller and Albert Einstein are living testimonies to those who made countermoves. For every choice, there is a consequence. True! But also remember, for every consequence, there is a counter choice. Be a choice maker and move ahead in life.

Every moment of life offers innumerable choices. For every choice I execute, I invite a consequence. While I have control over my choices, I can only have expectations over the consequences.

While I have a choice over choice, I am actually without choice about the consequence. While choices are born out of my intelligence, consequences are a feedback from

Existential Intelligence, the conglomeration of infinite forces known, unknown and unknowable. My microscopic intelligence operates out of the data at my disposal, while the macrocosmic intelligence operates out of Universal data.

Life progresses in the framework of choice-consequence-choice cycle. I execute a choice (I lead my life). Of course, the consequence of my choice is not in my control (I am being led). But again, how I respond to these consequences is once again my choice and that is in my control. My choices are my self-effort (X-axis). The consequences are my destiny (Y-axis). My future is neither completely controlled by consequences nor is it independent of my choices, but it is a resultant diagonal in the XY graph. Life is not Self-Effort Vs Destiny, but it is Self-Effort plus Destiny.

So, I will use my intelligence to execute choices. Surrender the same intelligence to the Existential Intelligence by faithfully accepting the consequences. And again use my intelligence to execute counter-choices to those consequences. On a yellow wall when I paint the blue, I will neither find the yellow nor get the blue, but a resultant green. However, if I continue my self-effort of painting the blue long enough, the wall will eventually turn blue.

So, if I don't get what I want in life, which I sometimes won't; if after all my efforts the results don't turn out to be what I aspired for, which they sometimes won't; if the consequences of my choices aren't what I intended, as they sometimes won't be... I will not lose my heart. Unintended consequences are life's way of showing me the possibilities I haven't thought about. Unintended consequences are Existence's way of telling me that it has a different plan for me... a plan larger than what I intended.

I will use the framework of choice-consequence-choice and keep progressing in life. Life is an 'I' plus 'Him' project, and not an 'I' versus 'Him' project.

Why nothing seems enough? What's the purpose of life?

Life is best lived when you don't try to demystify everything about life. You are not born for this or that! You are not here to book a place in the heaven or to have a coveted award bestowed upon you! You are here for the sheer joy of being useful; after all, the only other alternative is to be useless - to be used less.

Even if you do everything that you can do in life, still nothing will seem enough. So do you think the alternative is to give up everything and do nothing at all in life? Still you are not going to be at peace with yourself because life is not about how much you do or how little you do. Life is all about getting tossed between the paradoxical needs of 'having' and 'giving', and eventually gaining the maturity to discover the middle path. Your salvation is in discovering the middle path.

When the need to 'have' expresses itself, a person desires to possess. And, the selfishness within them gains expression. When the need to 'give' expresses itself, a person desires to share. And, the unselfishness within them finds expression. After all, you can give only what you have. So the need to 'have' always precedes the need to 'give'. The need to possess precedes the need to share. Every selfish individual will be unselfish at some time to somebody on some occasion.

No matter how much we achieve, there is a point at which all of us will once again feel like a failure. You run the race of life in laps only to discover that every finishing line is also the starting line. You run and run only to get back to where you started. The end of every lap is also the beginning of the next lap. As the success graph of life keeps soaring, you only realise, year after year that the closing balance once again becomes the opening balance, and you start all over again. The axis is always reset and you find yourself at '0, 0' on the graph of life, no matter how much you grow or how much you achieve. All these eventually leave you with the question, "Is this all worth it? What then is the purpose of life?"

Life isn't necessarily about a purpose, but it is about ensuring you add significance to everything and everybody you meet on the way. Whether you are useful or useless, the six feet beneath is reserved for all of us. After the game, the king and the pawn go into the same box. What we do for ourselves will die with us; what we do for others and for the world will be left behind and will remain immortal. There is no 'there' to reach. No end. No beginning. Life is just a perennial flow... Make it a useful flow. ●

“

The end of every lap is also the beginning of the next lap.

mahātria

11

Awareness and consciousness: Are they both the same or is one at a lower plane and the other is realised at a higher plane? Kindly elucidate.

What a blessing it is that a person can not only study a subject, but can also become the subject of their own study! What a gift that a person can study themselves! Hence these questions...

Awareness is a discipline. Consciousness is a happening. Awareness in the present continuous is consciousness. Consciousness with an element of past is awareness. And, it is through the doors of awareness that you attain the plane of consciousness. By practising the discipline of awareness you grow into being conscious.

How often we know 'what to do' before the incident and we also know 'what we should have done' after the incident. So, we are aware. Yet, we lose our alignment during the incident! So, we are not conscious. Being knowledgeable, before and after the incident, is just being aware. Only when they are bridged in the present continuous then you are conscious.

Firstly, awareness must be nurtured and developed by practicing introspection at the close of every day. Every day, before going to sleep, practice a mental run of all your experiences of that day. Recall each one of them. Pat yourself wherever you think you were right. Analyse your mistakes and ask yourself what else you could have done. Introspection helps you look into your actions and gain insight into your thoughts and feelings. Introspection will awaken your inner voice, which, in turn, will awaken you. You will find motivation to do more and more of what is right, and you will also discover through introspection that you are not repeating your mistakes.

Change the content of a thief and you have a Valmiki. A sinner is transformed into a saint by changing the contents of the being. An atma is transformed into a Mahatma when the content of the being is changed. When you become the subject of your own study through introspection, your self-judgement, self-observation and self-awareness will enable you to change the content of your very being. Introspection will bridge your knowing with your experiences.

With regular practice of this discipline of introspection and thus the resultant development of your self-awareness, you will reach a stage, when most of the events of your day will not need a post-mortem at the end of the day, but you will be aware of them as they happen through you. You have started becoming conscious... Yet, you will so often get tossed into your past or the future and thus lose being conscious in the present continuous... Keep working at it... Consciously, keep working at becoming conscious...

“

It is through
the doors of awareness
that you attain
the plane of consciousness.
By practising
the discipline of awareness
you grow into being conscious.

mahātria

12

I am tossed
between paradoxes,
all the time.
Why is it like this?

Three pairs of paradoxical needs drive human life. A person gets tossed between these paradoxical needs because when one need is satiated the other is starved. Then, you focus on satiating the latter, only to end up starving the former. Understand this paradox and you will understand life. And these paradoxical needs are,

1. Certainty and uncertainty.
2. Individuality and connectedness.
3. Having and giving.

First Paradox: Certainty provides order. Uncertainty provides growth. Both order and growth are needed to complete life. You want certainty. So, you try to achieve certainty by trying to control everything around you. Now, when your life becomes completely certain, when things become predictable, you become bored. So, while you want certainty, you simultaneously also want a certain amount of variety, which comes only out of uncertainty. You need surprises and challenges for you to feel fully alive. You again seek a degree of certainty. Two sides of the same coin but you keep toggling between the two sides, causing a rollercoaster ride in the flow and rhythm of your life...

Second Paradox: As a physical being you are the only one of your kind, absolutely unique and individualistic. But at the same time, as a spiritual being, the spirit of life that enlivens you is also the same spirit that enlivens all. So, spiritually you are connected to one and all. Both individuality and connectivity are needed to complete life. As a unique individual, you need identity. You need significance. Obviously, when your trumpet is too loud, others will begin to withdraw from you. That's why, you lose out on relationships; at least people begin to distance themselves. Now you feel lonely and isolated. So, you crave for connectedness. To meet this need, you join a fraternity or a club. Once you feel so well connected, you will again feel as if you have lost your own identity in a crowd. And, the seesaw of being tossed from one need to another only continues...

Third Paradox: Life is a flow and this flow is achieved through possessing and sharing. Both having and giving are needed to complete life. And, that's the third paradox. The need to have and the need to give. The need to consume and the need to contribute. And, the oscillation is between being spiritual in giving and being materialistic in having...

While everything you do will be tossed between these paradoxes, if you can find a few activities in your life, which fulfils all the six needs and gives you that balance in life, you will discover a new zeal in life... the kinds you have never experienced ever before. That's the secret to a complete life. ●

13

I believe God is omnipresent; then why should I visit temples?

In spirituality, there is an expression, "Spaces untouched by people." It refers to spaces that are untouched by the thoughts and feelings of human beings. That is, the existential vibrations with which that space came into existence, that space still carries the same vibrations. That's why, people went in search of the mountains, caves, deep jungles and a man swam across the ocean in search of an isolated rock island for their penance, seeking spaces untouched by any human being.

So, traditionally whenever enlightened people discovered a place with vibrations untouched by human beings, they initiated a place of worship, a temple, in that location, to create a space where people can come and inherit the vibrations of that place. In experiencing a space of high vibrations, long enough, you inherit the vibrations of that place. That is why it is foolish to argue, 'If God is omnipotent, omniscient and omnipresent, what is the necessity to go to places of worship'. God may be omnipresent, vibrations untouched by peoples aren't. They are concentrated only in a few places.

However, in the current scenario, where there is no space undiscovered or untouched by human beings, we seek the alternative. We seek spaces touched by the vibrations of the evolved souls.

While some spaces fill people with vibrations, some people fill spaces with vibrations. The idea behind inviting spiritually evolved people for the inauguration of new spaces, from temples to offices to homes, is because these people can fill spaces with their vibrations.

In fact, a spiritually evolved person, apart from all other characteristics, is one who remains attuned to vibrations of the highest frequency.

That's why it is said, where a spiritually evolved person sits, that space becomes a temple. "Where He sat became a temple" goes the Vedic saying.

Traditionally whenever enlightened people discovered a place with vibrations untouched by human beings, they initiated a place of worship, a temple, in that location, to create a space where people can come and inherit the vibrations of that place.

mahātria

Why should I meditate?

The science initially believed that all material is matter. The scientists then realised that matter is actually arrangement of atoms, which have a structure consisting of Nuclei made of protons and neutrons and electrons that seemed to have no structure. Later it was discovered that protons and neutrons are also made of smaller particles called quarks. And today science claims that all the particles, all the carriers of forces, are excitations of string-like objects. What is unifying and simple about a string is that all of the particles are all excitations of the same one object - the vibrating strings.

What science is able to explain today, spirituality had always explained that the more gross the matter, the lesser the frequency of vibrations; subtler the matter, higher the frequency of vibrations. Though the same vibrating strings constitute all matter, they resonate at different frequencies, depending on how gross or subtle the matter is. So the difference between the gross physical body and the subtler mind is only in the difference in the frequency of vibrations. So when you know how to tune into higher frequencies, you can tune into the thought flow of others. You can trade and share minds.

Why Meditation? Silence is basically vibrations with the highest frequency. Haven't you noticed, when the fan blades rotate at great speeds, they almost appear extinct? So, when the strings vibrate at their highest frequency, they almost seem like nothing, which is silence. However, it is from these highest vibrations all the relatively lower vibrations originate. Hence, the spiritual expression, everything comes from nothing. Everything is born out of silence.

However, vibrations are transferred only in a state of non-doing. That's the significance of you having to practice meditation, especially in places of worship or in the presence of an evolved soul. It enables you to inherit vibrations from that source. That's why you are asked not to speak in the presence of spiritually evolved people, for it isn't the time for doing, but it is time for non-doing. The power of non-doing is that it enables you to tune in and inherit the higher vibrations, and in the presence of higher vibrations, all things are possible. Everything is possible.

Even if you don't do anything else, meditate.

Meditation is not a technique learnt. It is something you grow into. Meditation is not added to you. It grows out of you. Meditation is not something you do. It is something you bring to what you do. ●

Vibrations are transferred only in a state of non-doing. That's the significance of you having to practice meditation, especially in places of worship or in the presence of an evolved soul.

mahātria

A young widowed mother
toiled alone to make him the VP.
He was just 35, survived by his
wife and a 4-year-old daughter.
Successful, no habits,
God-fearing, and peace loving...
One night he died in his sleep.
What is God's design in this?
Is God so cruel?

Some intelligence will ask the questions - like you. Some other intelligence will attempt to answer - like me. But, life and death are beyond Q and A. Life just moves on in its own order, way beyond what appears to be too random to our finite minds.

The pieces on the chessboard don't make the call. Whether to stay put or to move forward or to go back into the box - the player, who is playing the game, makes the call. The king or the pawn, you and I, are all mere pieces in an eternal game... By His call we came. By His call we will be in the game. By His call we will exit the game. And, by His call, we will re-enter the game, from a different starting position. The game just goes on... beyond your 'Q' and beyond my 'A'.

There is no rationale with which death can be explained. Human intelligence has the capacity to construct logic around anything... yet, no explanation, no rationale, no theory, and no logic is ever going to soothe the feelings of the heart, which bleeds at the loss of a loved one. And, even if there is truth in death, that truth makes no sense to a heart that is still drowning in its own emotions.

Time alone is the pain balm to an aching heart. With time, the emotions will shift from 'reeling at the loss of a loved one' to 'reliving the moments with the loved one'. In the past, you had your moments of laughter with them. In the present, unable to accept the loss, you cry by recalling those very moments. In the future, you will smile again reliving those very moments.

Emotionally, you always have a fresh introduction to yourself, with every passing day... with every passing moment, because your emotions are relevant just now.

Life incarnates with a form and a name, merely for the fulfilment of the soul. At 5 or 25 or 95, the soul departs from the body on its fulfilment. The soul embodied for a purpose, served its purpose, and having fulfilled its purpose, it moved on. Why will it continue to sit in the vehicle when the journey is over? Be happy for the soul that has attained its fulfilment.

We keep our relationships merely at the physical level and hence we suffer the physical loss. Shift the basis of your relationship from the physical plane to the spiritual plane. Physically, in bone and flesh, he was with you for 35 years. Spiritually, without a body and a name, now he will always be with you. 'Sometimes' has now become 'always'. So, please be happy for the soul that has attained its fulfilment. ●